The Teachings of Jesus

Ray Martinez

Library of Congress Control Number:		2023907344
ISBN:	Hardcover	978-1-6698-7412-6
	Softcover	978-1-6698-7413-3
	eBook	978-1-6698-7414-0

Print information available on the last page.

Rev. date: 04/19/2023

To order additional copies of this book, contact:
Xlibris
844-714-8691
www.Xlibris.com
Orders@Xlibris.com
852454

CONTENTS

PREFACE

I BELIEVE THAT JESUS Christ is the central figure of the Bible and that He was present in the Old Testament as well as the New Testament. Jesus was the promised Messiah who was prophesied in the Old Testament, and the entire Old Testament points to His coming.

One of the ways that Jesus is present in the Old Testament is through what is known as "Christophanies." These are appearances of Jesus Christ in various forms throughout the Old Testament. For example, in Genesis 18, three men visit Abraham, and it is believed by some that one of these men was Jesus Christ.

Another way that Jesus is present in the Old Testament is through prophecies that speak of His coming. For example, Isaiah 53 says that "He was pierced for our transgressions, he was crushed for our iniquities; the punishment that brought us peace was on him, and by his wounds we are healed."

These prophecies refer to Jesus, and they point to His coming as the Savior of the world.

In addition to Christophanies and prophecies, Jesus is present in the Old Testament through various types and shadows. For example, the sacrificial system outlined in the book of Leviticus is seen as a foreshadowing of Jesus's sacrifice on the cross.

The Old Testament points to Jesus through various types of people, such as Moses, who is seen as a type of Christ. Moses leads the Israelites out of slavery in Egypt, just as Jesus leads his people out of bondage to sin.

A Christophany is a pre-incarnate appearance of Jesus Christ in the Old Testament. Here are some examples of Christophanies in the Old Testament:

1. As I previously stated, in Genesis 18, three men visit Abraham, and one of them is believed to be Jesus Christ. Abraham refers to him as "my Lord" and "Adonai," which is a name for God.
2. In Genesis 32, Jacob wrestles with a man until daybreak. The man touches Jacob's hip and dislocates it, but Jacob refuses to let go until the man blesses him. The man then tells Jacob that his name will now be Israel, which means "one who struggles with God." It is believed that this man was Jesus Christ.
3. In Exodus 3, the burning bush appears to Moses, and God speaks to him from the bush. Some scholars believe that the angel of the Lord who appeared in the bush was Jesus Christ.
4. In Joshua 5, Joshua encounters a man with a drawn sword who identifies himself as the commander of the Lord's army. Joshua intentionally falls down and worships Him, and the man tells him to take off his sandals because he is standing on holy ground. Some scholars believe that this man was Jesus Christ.
5. In Daniel 3, Shadrach, Meshach, and Abednego are thrown into a fiery furnace for refusing to worship the golden statue of King Nebuchadnezzar. But they are not consumed by the fire, and a fourth figure appears in the furnace with them, who is described as "like a son of the gods." Some scholars believe that this fourth figure was Jesus Christ.
6. In the Bible, Melchizedek is considered a mysterious figure who is mentioned in Genesis 14 and Psalm 110.

> He is described as a king of Salem (which later became Jerusalem) and a priest of God Most High. He blesses Abraham, and Abraham gives him a tenth of everything he has.

In the New Testament, Melchizedek is mentioned again in the book of Hebrews. The author of Hebrews uses Melchizedek as an example to show that Jesus Christ is a high priest in the order of Melchizedek. The author argues that this makes Jesus superior to the Levitical priesthood of the Old Testament.

Hebrews 5:5–6 says, "So also Christ did not glorify himself in becoming a high priest, but was appointed by the one who said to him, 'You are my Son, today I have begotten you'; as he says also in another place, 'You are a priest forever, according to the order of Melchizedek.'"

Hebrews 7:1–3 says, "For this Melchizedek, king of Salem, priest of the Most High God, met Abraham returning from the slaughter of the kings and blessed him, and to him, Abraham apportioned a tenth part of everything. He is first, by translation of his name, king of righteousness, and then he is also king of Salem, that is, king of peace. He is without father or mother or genealogy and has neither beginning of days nor end of life, but resembling the Son of God he continues a priest forever."

Some scholars believe that Melchizedek may have been a Christophany, or a pre-incarnate appearance of Jesus Christ, which I believe is accurate. They point to the fact that Melchizedek is described as a priest of God Most High, and that he blesses Abraham in a way that only God can. They also point to the fact that the author of Hebrews compares Jesus to Melchizedek, suggesting that there is a deeper connection between the two.

However, not all scholars believe that Melchizedek was a Christophany. Some believe that he was a historical figure who was simply used as an example in the book of Hebrews to make a theological point about Jesus Christ.

While some scholars believe that Melchizedek was a Christophany, it is not a universally accepted belief. The exact nature of Melchizedek remains a mystery, and his significance lies in his role as an example of the high priesthood of Jesus Christ.

These are just a few examples of Christophanies in the Old Testament. There are many more instances where Jesus Christ is believed to have appeared in some form or another.

There is not a definitive list of scholars who believe that Melchizedek is a Christophany, as this is a matter of interpretation and not a universally accepted belief. However, some notable scholars who have suggested the possibility of Melchizedek being a Christophany include:

1. F.F. Bruce - Bruce was a respected biblical scholar and theologian who wrote extensively on the New Testament and the book of Hebrews in particular. In his commentary on Hebrews, he suggests that Melchizedek may have been a pre-incarnate appearance of Christ.
2. John MacArthur - MacArthur is a prominent pastor and author who has written extensively on the Bible and theology. In his sermon series on Hebrews, he suggests that Melchizedek may have been a Christophany based on the similarities between Melchizedek and Christ as high priests.
3. James Coffman - Coffman was a respected biblical commentator who wrote a commentary on the book of Hebrews. In his commentary, he suggests that Melchizedek may have been a pre-incarnate appearance of Christ based on his unique characteristics and the way he is described in the Bible.

4. John Gill - Gill was an eighteenth-century theologian and biblical scholar who wrote a commentary on the entire Bible. In his commentary on Hebrews, he suggests that Melchizedek may have been a Christophany based on his eternal priesthood and his resemblance to Christ as a priest.

In summary, I believe that Jesus is present in the Old Testament in various ways, including through Christophanies, prophecies, types and shadows, and types of people. I think that the entire Old Testament points to Jesus as the promised Messiah and savior of the world from the beginning to the end of the Bible. Even when we take the sacraments, Christ is ever so present.

ACKNOWLEDGMENTS

MY DEEPEST GRATITUDE to the people who have helped me on my life's journey. To my mentors, counselors, and advisors, who have provided me with guidance, wisdom, and support, I am forever grateful. Your kindness, understanding, and unwavering support have been a source of comfort and inspiration to me. Through your patient listening, thoughtful advice, and gentle encouragement, you have given me the strength and courage to face life's challenges and pursue my dreams.

Thank you for your generous and selfless spirit, for taking the time to invest in my life, and for believing in me even when I didn't believe in myself. Your unwavering faith in me has been a beacon of hope and a guiding light on my journey.

As I continue to navigate the twists and turns of life, I will always carry your words of wisdom and your loving presence in my heart. Thank you for being a part of my life and for sharing your gifts with me. I am truly blessed to have you in my life.

Becky Cisneros
Luke McFetridge
Gino Campana and the entire family
Jorge Hernandez (Coco)
Ken Borrett
Darin and Debra Atteberry
Gerry and Cindy Agnes
Juan and Alexandria Campana
The Smotherman family
The Tuesday morning Timberline men's study group
The Wednesday morning businessmen's study group

Wil and Pam Nation and the entire Ager family
Ross and Gloria B. Ager (my biological mother and step father)
Delores Mata
The Gomez family
Jeff Swoboda, FCPD Chief of Police
Adam and Tiffany Vartanyan
Lloyd Garcia (US Olympic Champion in weight lifting)
Gil Carbajal, PhD
Coach Hal Kinard
Lewis and Pearl Martinez (my adopted parents)
Jonathan and Charlotte Moore
Jay and Rodney Moore
Nadine Trijillo-Rogers
Sarah Kane

My gratitude goes to Thaylor Iron Rope for the inspiring quotes from his book. His words have provided me with the inspiration and motivation I needed to pursue my dreams and goals. Thaylor's words have resonated with me deeply and have given me the courage to face life's challenges with grace and resilience. His wisdom and intuitiveness are truly a gift to the world, and I am thankful to have read your book. Thank you for sharing your gifts with the world and for being a source of inspiration to so many.

***

"If I live for myself, I die with dishonor, but if I live for Christ I die with honor."

"God created faith and man, made religion."

"There is only one way to heaven and a lot of ways to hell!"

"Don't bring the world into church; bring the church into the world."

"Lord, may I never depart from You, but always be a part of You."

***

Quotes are used with permission from Thaylor Iron Rope in his book, *The Book of Service*.

INTRODUCTION

THE TEACHINGS OF Jesus Christ have been a source of inspiration and guidance for countless individuals for over two thousand years. His message of love, compassion, and forgiveness has touched the hearts of people all over the world, and His teachings continue to provide wisdom and insight for those seeking a deeper understanding of life and spiritual truth.

In this book, we will explore the teachings of Jesus as recorded in the Bible, with a focus on His core messages and timeless principles. We will examine His teachings on love, forgiveness, humility, faith, and more, and consider how they apply to our lives today.

Through the words of Jesus, we will discover the transformative power of His teachings, and gain a deeper appreciation for His life and mission. Whether you are a longtime follower of Jesus or simply curious about His teachings, this book offers a fresh perspective on His message and its relevance to our lives today.

May the teachings of Jesus fill your heart with hope, peace, and joy, and inspire you to live a life of love, service, and spiritual growth. The following is a poem I created for this book, *The Teachings of Jesus.*

The teachings of Jesus, so pure and true,
Bring light and hope to me and you,
With gentle words and loving grace,
He guides us to a better place.

He spoke of love, the greatest command,
To love our neighbor, hand in hand,
To love our enemies, forgive and bless,
And in doing so, find true happiness.

He taught of faith, a mustard seed,
That moves mountains and meets our needs,
To trust in God and His great plan,
And know that all things are in His hand.

He showed us how to live with grace,
To humble ourselves in every place,
To serve and give with a joyful heart,
And in doing so, find our true part.

And in His life, He paved the way,
To show us how to live each day,
With compassion, kindness, and selfless love,
A reflection of our Father above.

So let us heed His teachings true,
And let His love shine through and through,
For in following His holy way,
We find true life and hope each day.

CHAPTER 1

Jesus Cares

IN THIS CHAPTER, we will explore the theme of Jesus's care for His followers. Throughout the Bible, we see evidence of His love and concern for those who believe in Him. From healing the sick to comforting the broken-hearted, Jesus demonstrates His compassion in numerous ways. In this chapter, we will explore some of the key biblical references that highlight just how much Jesus cares for us.

Jesus cares for the sick: One of the most well-known examples of Jesus's care for the sick is found in Mark 1:40–42, where He heals a man with leprosy. The man approaches Jesus and begs Him to make him clean. Despite the social stigma surrounding lepers, Jesus reaches out and touches the man, telling him, "I am willing. Be clean!" The man is immediately healed, and Jesus instructs him to go show himself to the priest.

This story highlights Jesus's willingness to show compassion to those who are suffering from physical ailments. He doesn't turn away from those who are considered outcasts by society, but instead, He touches them and heals them. This is a powerful reminder that Jesus cares for us, no matter what our circumstances may be.

Jesus cares for the broken-hearted: In Psalm 34:18, we read that "the Lord is close to the brokenhearted and saves those who are crushed in spirit." This verse is a powerful reminder that Jesus cares for those who are struggling emotionally. Whether we are dealing with grief, anxiety, or depression, Jesus is there for us. He offers comfort and hope to those who are hurting, and He promises to never leave us or forsake us (Heb. 13:5).

One of the most poignant examples of Jesus's care for the broken-hearted is found in John 11:35–36, where He weeps over the death of His friend Lazarus. Even though Jesus knows that he is going to raise Lazarus from the dead, He is still deeply moved by the pain and sorrow of those around Him. This is a beautiful example of how Jesus identifies with our pain and is there for us in our darkest moments.

Jesus cares for those who are lost: In Luke 15:3–7, Jesus tells the parable of the lost sheep. He explains that if a shepherd has one hundred sheep and one of them wanders off, He will leave the ninety-nine and go after the lost sheep until He finds it. This story is a powerful reminder that Jesus cares for those who are lost and wandering. He is willing to leave everything behind to search for us and bring us back into His fold.

This theme of Jesus's care for the lost is echoed throughout the New Testament. In Luke 19:10, Jesus tells us that He came to seek and save the lost. He doesn't give up on us when we stray from His path, but instead, He pursues us relentlessly. This is a powerful reminder of just how much Jesus cares for us, even when we don't deserve it.

Conclusion: Throughout the Bible, we see evidence of Jesus's care and compassion for His followers. Whether we are sick, broken-hearted, or lost, He is there for us, offering comfort, healing, and hope. As we strive to follow in His footsteps, may we also show care and compassion to those around us, reflecting the love of Christ to a hurting world.

Even through my personal journey in life, there is no doubt that Jesus cares. He has lifted me up so many times and redirected my life to a better path than I ever imagined. What I thought was good wasn't, and what I thought was impossible became possible. I no longer have to believe in Jesus; I know Him beyond a shadow of a doubt.

CHAPTER 2

What Jesus Doesn't Care About

IN MANY WAYS, Jesus is a polarizing figure. His teachings and actions have inspired millions of people throughout history, but they have also been the source of controversy and debate. As we look at the life of Jesus, we can see that there are certain things that He didn't care about. In this chapter, we will explore some of these aspects of Jesus's life and teachings.

Jesus doesn't care about material possessions: Throughout His teachings, Jesus emphasizes the importance of living a simple and humble life. He warns His followers against the dangers of greed and materialism, urging them to focus instead on spiritual wealth (Matt. 6:19–21). He doesn't care about accumulating wealth or possessions, but instead, He encourages His followers to give generously to those in need (Luke 12:33–34).

This is exemplified in the story of the rich young ruler in Mark 10:17–27. The young man asks Jesus what he must do to inherit eternal life, and Jesus tells him to sell all his possessions and give the money to the poor. The young man is unable to do this, and Jesus tells His disciples that it is easier for a camel to go through the eye of a needle than for a rich person to enter the kingdom of God.

Jesus doesn't care about social status: In a culture where social status is highly valued, Jesus shows no favoritism based on a person's position in society. He eats with tax collectors and sinners (Matthew 9:10–13), heals the sick and the outcasts (Luke 17:11–19), and speaks out against the religious leaders who place their own social status above serving God (Matt. 23:1–12).

In fact, Jesus often challenges the social norms of His day. He speaks to women and Samaritans, both of whom are considered second-class citizens in Jewish society. In John 4:7–30, Jesus speaks with a Samaritan woman at a well, breaking down cultural barriers and showing that he doesn't care about social status.

Jesus doesn't care about outward appearances: While the religious leaders of Jesus's day place great importance on outward appearances, Jesus emphasizes the importance of inner purity. He criticizes the Pharisees for their hypocrisy, saying that they look good on the outside but are full of greed and self-indulgence on the inside (Matthew 23:25–28).

Jesus also doesn't care about physical appearances or disabilities. He heals the blind, the lame, and the lepers, showing that He values people for who they are on the inside rather than their physical appearance (Matt. 9:27-31, John 9:1–7).

Conclusion: As we look at the life of Jesus, we can see that there are certain things that he doesn't care about. He doesn't care about accumulating wealth or possessions, social status, or outward appearances. Instead, He emphasizes the importance of living a simple and humble life, serving others, and focusing on inner purity. As we strive to follow in His footsteps, may we also let go of the things that don't matter and focus on what truly does: loving God and loving others.

CHAPTER 3

How Jesus Reasons with People

JESUS IS KNOWN for His ability to reason with people, using logic and wisdom to engage with them and challenge their beliefs. He often uses parables and analogies to communicate complex concepts in a way that was easy to understand. In this chapter, we will explore some key examples of how Jesus reasons with people.

Jesus uses parables to communicate complex concepts: One of the most effective ways that Jesus reasons with people is through the use of parables. These simple stories often have a deeper meaning that challenges people to think more deeply about their beliefs and actions. For example, in Matthew 13:1–9, Jesus tells the parable of the sower, which illustrates the different ways that people respond to the message of the Gospel.

Another example is found in Luke 10:25–37, where Jesus tells the parable of the good Samaritan. This story challenges the listener to rethink their prejudices and biases, showing that true compassion transcends cultural and social barriers.

Jesus uses questions to challenge assumptions: Another effective way that Jesus reasons with people is by asking questions that challenge their assumptions. In Matthew 22:15–22, the Pharisees try to trap Jesus by asking Him whether it is lawful to pay taxes to Caesar. Jesus responds by asking for a coin and then asking whose image is on it. When they answer that it is

Caesar's, Jesus tells them to give to Caesar what is Caesar's and to give to God what is God's.

In John 8:1–11, the religious leaders bring a woman caught in adultery to Jesus, asking Him what they should do with her. Jesus responds by writing on the ground and then saying, "Let any one of you who is without sin be the first to throw a stone at her." This challenges their assumptions about their own righteousness and forces them to confront their own sinfulness.

Jesus uses analogies to make concepts accessible: Finally, Jesus often uses analogies to help people understand complex concepts. For example, in John 10:7–18, Jesus uses the analogy of a shepherd and His sheep to describe His relationship with His followers. He says that He is the good shepherd who lays down His life for his sheep, illustrating the depth of His love and sacrifice.

In Matthew 13:31–32, Jesus uses the analogy of a mustard seed to describe the kingdom of God. He says that even though it is small, it grows into a large tree that provides shelter for many. This illustrates the power and potential of the kingdom of God, even though it may seem insignificant at first.

Conclusion: Throughout His ministry, Jesus reasons with people in a variety of ways, using parables, questions, and analogies to challenge their beliefs and open their hearts to the truth. As we seek to share the Gospel with others, we can learn from His example, using these same techniques to communicate complex concepts in a way that is accessible and engaging. May we follow in His footsteps as we seek to share the love of Christ with the world.

In my personal journey, Jesus sure asks me a lot of questions that cause me to ponder and pause. I'm sure glad I listened to His questions.

CHAPTER 4

What Jesus Says About Love

LOVE IS A central theme in the teachings of Jesus. He emphasizes the importance of loving God and loving others, and his own life is a shining example of sacrificial love. In this chapter, we will explore some key examples of what Jesus says about love.

Love God with all your heart: One of the most important commandments that Jesus gives is to love God with all your heart, soul, mind, and strength. In Mark 12:28–34, a scribe asks Jesus which commandment is the most important. Jesus responds by quoting from Deuteronomy 6:4–5, saying, "Hear, O Israel: The Lord our God, the Lord is one. Love the Lord your God with all your heart and with all your soul and with all your mind and with all your strength."

This commandment emphasizes the importance of having a deep and authentic love for God, one that encompasses every aspect of our being. When we love God in this way, we are able to love others more fully as well.

Love your neighbor as yourself: Another key commandment that Jesus gives is to love your neighbor as yourself. In Mark 12:28–34, Jesus goes on to say that this commandment is like the first, in that it sums up all the other commandments. He says, "There is no commandment greater than these."

This commandment emphasizes the importance of loving others in the same way that we love ourselves. It means treating others with kindness, compassion, and respect, and seeking to meet their needs just as we would our own. This kind of love is not based on what we can get from others, but rather on what we can give to them.

Love Your Enemies: Perhaps one of the most challenging teachings that Jesus gives is to love your enemies. In Matthew 5:43–48, Jesus says, "You have heard that it was said, 'Love your neighbor and hate your enemy.' But I tell you, love your enemies and pray for those who persecute you, that you may be children of your Father in heaven."

This kind of love goes beyond the natural inclination to love those who love us in return. It means extending love and grace even to those who have hurt us or sought to do us harm. It is a radical kind of love that reflects the selfless, sacrificial love that Jesus shows on the cross.

Conclusion: Throughout His teachings, Jesus emphasizes the importance of love. He teaches us to love God with all our heart, soul, mind, and strength, to love our neighbors as ourselves, and even to love our enemies. This kind of love is not based on what we can get from others, but rather on what we can give to them. As we seek to follow in His footsteps, may we learn to love as He loved, and to show the world the transformative power of sacrificial love.

For me, what this boils down to is if I can't love myself, my neighbors, and strangers, then I cannot love Jesus. How can I not love others whom God created in His image? When I look at people, I see the creation of the Creator. Yes, some people destroy His creation, but God can reshape and reform them.

CHAPTER 5

What Jesus Says About Grace

GRACE IS A central theme in the teachings of Jesus. He emphasizes the importance of receiving God's grace and extending it to others. Let's explore some key examples of what Jesus says about grace.

Grace for sinners: One of the most significant messages that Jesus proclaims is that God's grace is available to all, regardless of their past mistakes or sins. In Luke 15:11–32, Jesus tells the parable of the prodigal son, which illustrates the depth and breadth of God's grace. The son, who had squandered his inheritance and lived a life of sin, returns home to his father, who welcomes him back with open arms. This parable shows that no matter how far we may have strayed from God, His grace is always available to us when we turn back to Him.

In Matthew 9:9—13, Jesus calls Matthew, a tax collector, to be one of His disciples. The religious leaders of the day criticized Jesus for associating with tax collectors and sinners, but Jesus responds by saying, "It is not the healthy who need a doctor, but the sick. But go and learn what this means: 'I desire mercy, not sacrifice.' For I have not come to call the righteous, but sinners." This shows that Jesus came to offer grace and forgiveness to those who recognize their need for it.

Grace for the unworthy: Another important aspect of Jesus's message of grace is that it is available to all, regardless of their status or worthiness. In Luke 7:36–50, Jesus is invited to the home of a Pharisee named Simon. While he is there, a woman who is known to be a sinner comes in and washes Jesus's feet with her tears and perfume. Simon is critical of her actions, but Jesus responds by saying, "Therefore, I tell you, her many sins have been forgiven—as her great love has shown. But whoever has been forgiven little loves little." This shows that even those who are considered unworthy by society can receive God's grace.

Grace for all: Finally, Jesus emphasizes that God's grace is available to all, regardless of their background or circumstances. In Matthew 22:1–14, Jesus tells the parable of the wedding banquet, in which a king invites guests to his son's wedding feast. When the first guests refuse to come, the king invites anyone who will come, both good and bad. This shows that God's grace is not limited to a select few, but is offered to all who accept His invitation.

Conclusion: Throughout His teachings, Jesus emphasizes the importance of receiving and extending God's grace. He shows that no matter how far we may have strayed from God, His grace is always available to us when we turn back to Him. He also shows that God's grace is not limited to a select few but is offered to all who accept His invitation. As we seek to follow in his footsteps, may we extend grace and love to those around us, just as He has extended it to us.

Grace is receiving something we don't deserve.

CHAPTER 6

What Jesus Says About Mercy

MERCY IS A central theme in the teachings of Jesus. He emphasizes the importance of showing mercy to others and receiving God's mercy in our own lives. In this chapter, we will explore some key examples of what Jesus says about mercy.

Showing mercy to others: One of the most important teachings that Jesus gives is to show mercy to others. In Matthew 5:7, He says, "Blessed are the merciful, for they will be shown mercy." This beatitude emphasizes the importance of extending kindness, compassion, and forgiveness to others, even when they do not deserve it.

In Luke 10:25–37, Jesus tells the parable of the good Samaritan, which illustrates the importance of showing mercy to those in need, regardless of their social status or background. The Samaritan, who was considered an outcast by the Jews, stops to help a man who had been beaten and left for dead, while the religious leaders of the day pass by without offering assistance. This parable shows that true mercy is not limited by social or cultural boundaries, but is offered to all who are in need.

Receiving God's mercy: Another important aspect of Jesus's message of mercy is that we have all received God's mercy in our own lives. In Luke 18:9–14, Jesus tells the parable of the Pharisee and the tax collector. The Pharisee boasts about his own righteousness, while the tax collector humbly asks for

God's mercy, saying, "God, have mercy on me, a sinner." Jesus says that the tax collector, not the Pharisee, goes home justified because he recognizes his own need for mercy.

In Matthew 9:9–13, Jesus calls Matthew, a tax collector, to be one of His disciples. The religious leaders of the day criticized Jesus for associating with tax collectors and sinners, but Jesus responds by saying, "I desire mercy, not sacrifice. For I have not come to call the righteous, but sinners." This shows that no matter how far we may have strayed from God, His mercy is always available to us when we turn back to Him.

Conclusion: Throughout His teachings, Jesus emphasizes the importance of showing mercy to others and receiving God's mercy in our own lives. He shows that true mercy is not limited by social or cultural boundaries but is offered to all who are in need. As we seek to follow in His footsteps, may we extend mercy and love to those around us, just as He has extended it to us.

Think of mercy in this way: It's God putting Himself in our shoes. If we could just walk a mile in someone else's shoes, we begin to understand God's mercifulness.

CHAPTER 7

What Jesus Says About Depression and Loneliness

DEPRESSION AND LONELINESS are common struggles that many people face. But what does Jesus have to say about these difficult emotions? We will explore some key examples of what Jesus says about depression and loneliness.

Jesus's own experience with sorrow: Before looking at what Jesus says about depression and loneliness, it is important to note that He experiences these emotions Himself. In Matthew 26:36–38, Jesus goes to the garden of Gethsemane to pray before His arrest and crucifixion. He tells His disciples, "My soul is overwhelmed with sorrow to the point of death. Stay here and keep watch with me." This shows that even Jesus, the Son of God, experiences deep sorrow and anguish.

Jesus's response to depression and loneliness: One of the most important messages that Jesus gives about depression and loneliness is that we are never truly alone. In Matthew 28:20, he says, "And surely I am with you always, to the very end of the age." This promise of His presence reminds us that even in our darkest moments, we are not alone.

In John 14:18, Jesus says, "I will not leave you as orphans; I will come to you." This assurance of His love and care for us reminds us that we are not abandoned but are deeply loved by Him.

In Luke 4:18, Jesus quotes the prophet, Isaiah, saying, "The Spirit of the Lord is on me because he has anointed me to proclaim good news to the poor. He has sent me to proclaim freedom for the prisoners and recovery of sight for the blind, to set the oppressed free." This shows that Jesus comes to bring hope and healing to those who are struggling, including those who are experiencing depression and loneliness.

Conclusion: While depression and loneliness can be difficult to bear, Jesus offers hope and comfort to those who are struggling. His promise of His presence reminds us that we are never truly alone, and His message of hope and healing offers a way forward. May we turn to Him in our moments of darkness and find comfort and strength in His love and care.

All of us have experienced dark moments in our life—whether the incidents are from embarrassment, shame, defeat, victimization of crime, divorce, or loneliness—we have a resource from the comforter that Jesus sent us.

CHAPTER 8

What Does Jesus Mean When He Says That the Truth Will Set You Free?

THE STATEMENT "THE truth will set you free" is one of the most well-known sayings of Jesus. But what does He mean by this? In this chapter, we will explore the context and meaning behind this powerful statement.

The context of Jesus's statement: In John 8:31–32, Jesus is speaking to a group of Jews who believed in him. He says, "If you hold to my teaching, you are really my disciples. Then you will know the truth, and the truth will set you free." This statement comes in the context of a conversation about freedom and slavery, with the Jews pointing out that they have never been slaves to anyone. Jesus responds by saying that everyone who sins is a slave to sin.

The meaning of Jesus's statement: So what does Jesus mean when He says that the truth will set you free? One interpretation is that He is referring to the truth about Himself—that He is the way, the truth, and the life (John 14:6). Knowing the truth about who He is and what He has done for us through His death and resurrection can set us free from the power of sin and death.

Another interpretation is that Jesus is referring to the truth about ourselves. When we face the truth about our own sin and brokenness, we can find freedom in the forgiveness and grace that Jesus offers. As we confess our sins and turn to him, He sets us free from the guilt and shame that can weigh us down.

Finally, Jesus may have been referring to the truth about the world around us. When we seek the truth and understand the reality of the brokenness and injustice in the world, we can be inspired to work for justice and freedom for all. In this way, the truth can set us free to live for a greater purpose beyond ourselves.

Conclusion: The statement "the truth will set you free" is a powerful reminder of the freedom that Jesus offers to all who follow Him. Whether we are seeking the truth about ourselves, about Jesus, or about the world around us, His promise of freedom rings true. May we hold fast to His teaching, seek the truth with open hearts and minds, and find the freedom that He offers.

Jesus is the truth.

CHAPTER 9

What Jesus Wants from Us

AS CHRISTIANS, WE often ask ourselves what Jesus wants from us. We will explore some key aspects of what Jesus desires from His followers.

Love God: Jesus makes it clear that the greatest commandment is to love God with all our heart, soul, mind, and strength (Mark 12:30). This means putting God first in our lives and seeking to honor Him in all we do. We are called to love Him through worship, prayer, and obedience to His commands.

Love others: Jesus also commands us to love our neighbors as ourselves (Mark 12:31). This means loving and caring for others as we would want to be loved and cared for. Jesus calls us to show compassion and kindness to all, even our enemies (Matthew 5:44).

Follow Him: Jesus's call to "follow me" (Matt. 4:19) is a call to a life of discipleship. We are called to follow His example of love, compassion, and sacrifice. This means living a life that reflects His teachings and character and seeking to share His love with others.

Serve others: Jesus teaches that the greatest among us is the one who serves (Matthew 23:11). He demonstrated this by washing His disciples' feet and ultimately laying down His life for us. Jesus calls us to serve others in His name, using our gifts and talents to meet the needs of those around us.

Obey His commands: Jesus says, "If you love me, keep my commands" (John 14:15). This means that our love for Jesus should result in obedience to His teachings. We are called to follow His example of humility, forgiveness, and love, and to live a life that honors Him.

Conclusion: Jesus wants us to love God, love others, follow Him, serve others, and obey His commands. These are not just empty commands but are the keys to a life of purpose and meaning. May we seek to live a life that reflects His teachings and character, and may we be empowered by the Holy Spirit to live out His call on our lives.

Christ accepted us a long time ago. It's up to us to accept Him. When kids are adopted in front of the courts, the judge always asked the parents if they accept this child. And then the children, if they're of age of understanding, are always asked if they accept their parents.

God says, "Tell me personally if you want to accept me. We don't have to be in the halls of justice, but only in the pathway of Christ." This really demonstrates His love. God loves you and wants you to know Him so He can fill you with peace and give you a real life—forever.

"Even before he made the world, God loved us and chose us in Christ to be holy and without fault in his eyes. God decided in advance to adopt us into his own family by bringing us to himself through Jesus Christ. This is what he wanted to do, and it gave him great pleasure" (Ephesians 1:4–5 NLT).

CHAPTER 10

What Jesus Says About Temptation

TEMPTATION IS SOMETHING that every human being faces, and it can be difficult to resist. In this chapter, we will explore what Jesus had to say about temptation and how we can follow his example in resisting it.

Jesus's temptation in the wilderness: Before we look at what Jesus says about temptation, it is important to note that he himself faces temptation. In Matthew 4:1–11, Jesus is led by the Spirit into the wilderness to be tempted by the devil. Each time the devil tempts him, Jesus responds with Scripture, ultimately resisting the devil's schemes.

What Jesus says about temptation: In Matthew 26:41, Jesus tells His disciples to "watch and pray so that you will not fall into temptation. The spirit is willing, but the flesh is weak." This shows that Jesus understands the power of temptation and the need for vigilance in resisting it.

In Luke 22:40, Jesus tells His disciples to pray that they will not fall into temptation. This shows that prayer is a powerful tool in resisting temptation, as we can ask God for strength and guidance in the face of temptation.

In Matthew 5:29–30, Jesus says, "If your right eye causes you to stumble, gouge it out and throw it away. It is better for you to lose one part of your body than for your whole body to be thrown into hell." This extreme language shows the seriousness of temptation and the need to take drastic measures to avoid it.

How we can follow Jesus's example: So how can we follow Jesus's example in resisting temptation? Here are a few ways:

1. Know the scripture. Just as Jesus uses the scripture to resist the devil's temptations, we can also use the Bible to help us resist temptation. Memorizing key verses and meditating on them can help us stay focused on God's truth.
2. Pray. Like Jesus's disciples, we can pray for strength and guidance in the face of temptation. Asking God to help us resist temptation can make all the difference.
3. Avoid triggers. Jesus's extreme language in Matthew 5:29–30 shows that sometimes we need to take drastic measures to avoid temptation. This might mean avoiding certain people, places, or activities that are likely to lead us into temptation.

Conclusion: Temptation is a powerful force in our lives, but Jesus has shown us how to resist it. By knowing the scripture, praying, and avoiding triggers, we can follow His example and stay faithful to God in the face of temptation. May we seek His guidance and strength as we face the challenges of temptation in our lives.

"No temptation has overtaken you except what is common to mankind. And God is faithful; he will not let you be tempted beyond what you can bear. But when you are tempted, he will also provide a way out so that you can endure it" 1 Cor. 10:13, NIV.

CHAPTER 11

What Jesus Says About the End Times

THE TOPIC OF the end times has fascinated people for centuries. In this chapter, we will explore what Jesus has to say about the end times and what we can learn from His teachings.

Jesus's teachings on the end times: In Matthew 24, Jesus gives a lengthy discourse about the end times. He warns His disciples about false prophets, wars and rumors of wars, famines, earthquakes, and persecution. He also speaks of the coming of the Son of Man, saying that no one knows the day or the hour of His return.

In Mark 13, Jesus again speaks of the end times, warning His disciples to be on guard and to stay awake. He speaks of the coming of the Son of Man and the signs that will precede His return.

In Luke 21, Jesus speaks of the destruction of the temple in Jerusalem and the signs that will precede His return. He warns His disciples to be on guard and not be weighed down by the worries of life.

What we can learn from Jesus's teachings:

1. Be on guard. Jesus's repeated warnings to be on guard and to stay awake show that we need to be vigilant in our faith. We should not be complacent or apathetic but

should be actively seeking to grow in our relationship with God and to share His love with others.

2. Persevere through trials. Jesus's warnings of persecution and hardship show that we will face trials in this life. However, He also promises that those who persevere to the end will be saved (Matthew 24:13).
3. Trust in God's timing. Jesus's statement that no one knows the day or the hour of His return shows that we should not be preoccupied with trying to predict when the end will come. Instead, we should trust in God's timing and focus on living a faithful life.
4. Share the Gospel. Jesus's teachings on the end times should motivate us to share the Gospel with others. We should be actively seeking to help others come to faith in Jesus so that they too can be saved.

Conclusion: Jesus's teachings on the end times can be both sobering and encouraging. They remind us of the reality of trials and persecution in this life, but also of the hope we have in Christ's return. May we be on guard, persevere through trials, trust in God's timing, and share the Gospel with others as we await His coming.

CHAPTER 12

What Jesus Says About the Rapture

THE TOPIC OF rapture has been a point of debate among Christians for many years. In this chapter, we will explore what Jesus has to say about the rapture and what we can learn from His teachings.

What is the rapture? The term "rapture" comes from the Latin word *rapturo*, which means "to catch up." The rapture is a concept in Christian eschatology that refers to an event in which believers in Jesus Christ will be caught up in the air to meet Him upon His return.

What Jesus says about the rapture: While Jesus does not specifically use the term rapture, He does speak about the events that will take place upon His return. In Matthew 24:30–31, Jesus says, "Then will appear the sign of the Son of Man in heaven. And then all the peoples of the earth will mourn when they see the Son of Man coming on the clouds of heaven, with power and great glory. And he will send his angels with a loud trumpet call, and they will gather his elect from the four winds, from one end of the heavens to the other."

This passage speaks of a gathering of believers from all over the world, which could be interpreted as a reference to the rapture. Jesus also speaks of the coming of the Son of Man in Mark 13:26–27, saying, "At that time people will see the Son of Man coming in clouds with great power and glory. And he will send his angels and gather his elect from the four winds, from the ends of the earth to the ends of the heavens."

What we can learn from Jesus's teachings:

1. The rapture is a real event. While Jesus did not use the term "rapture," His teachings make it clear that there will be a gathering of believers upon His return.
2. Our response matters: In Matthew 24:42, Jesus says, "Therefore keep watch, because you do not know on what day your Lord will come." This shows that we should be prepared for Christ's return and live a faithful life.
3. We will be with Jesus forever. In 1 Thessalonians 4:17, Paul speaks of believers being caught up in the air to meet the Lord, and then being with Him forever. This shows that the rapture is a moment of great joy for believers, as we will be with Jesus for eternity.

Conclusion: The rapture is a topic that has caused much discussion and debate among Christians, but Jesus's teachings make it clear that there will be a gathering of believers upon His return. May we be prepared for that day, living faithfully and looking forward to the joy of being with Jesus forever.

CHAPTER 13

Asking, Seeking, and Knocking: What Jesus Says About Prayer

PRAYER IS AN integral part of the Christian faith. We will explore what Jesus had to say about prayer, specifically about asking, seeking, and knocking.

What Jesus says about asking, seeking, and knocking: In Matthew 7:7–8, Jesus says, "Ask and it will be given to you; seek and you will find; knock and the door will be opened to you. For everyone who asks receives; the one who seeks finds; and to the one who knocks, the door will be opened."

These words are a call to persistent prayer and trust in God's provision. Jesus is saying that we should not give up on our prayers, but rather, we should continue to ask, seek, and knock. He also promises that our prayers will be answered.

In Luke 11:9–10, Jesus repeats this call to persistent prayer, saying, "So I say to you: Ask and it will be given to you; seek and you will find; knock and the door will be opened to you. For everyone who asks receives; the one who seeks finds; and to the one who knocks, the door will be opened."

What we can learn from Jesus's teachings:

1. We should pray with persistence. Jesus's call to ask, seek, and knock is a call to persistent prayer. We should

not give up on our prayers but continue to bring our requests before God.

2. We can trust in God's provision. Jesus promises that our prayers will be answered. While the answer may not always be what we expect or want, we can trust that God will provide for our needs.
3. Prayer is a relationship with God. Jesus's teachings on prayer remind us that prayer is not just a list of requests but a relationship with God. We should come to God with a humble and open heart, seeking to know Him more deeply.

Conclusion: Jesus's teachings on asking, seeking, and knocking are a call to persistent prayer and trust in God's provision. May we approach prayer with humility, persistence, and trust, knowing that our God is faithful and will answer our prayers according to His will.

CHAPTER 14

How Jesus Teaches Us to Pray

PRAYER IS A vital part of the Christian faith, and Jesus taught His disciples how to pray. In this chapter, we will explore what Jesus says about how we should pray.

What Jesus says about prayer: In Matthew 6:5–15, Jesus gives His disciples guidance on how to pray. He begins by warning them not to pray to be seen by others, but rather to pray in secret. He then gives them an example of how to pray, which is commonly known as the Lord's Prayer.

The Lord's Prayer goes as follows:

Our Father in heaven,
hallowed be your name,
your kingdom come,
your will be done,
on earth as it is in heaven.
Give us today our daily bread.
And forgive us our debts,
as we also have forgiven our debtors.
And lead us not into temptation,
but deliver us from the evil one.

What we can learn from Jesus's teaching:

1. Prayer should be humble. Jesus warns His disciples not to pray to be seen by others. We should come to God with a humble heart, recognizing our need for Him.

2. Prayer should be focused on God's will. In the Lord's Prayer, Jesus teaches His disciples to pray for God's will to be done on earth as it is in heaven. Our prayers should be focused on God's will and not our own desires.
3. Prayer should be daily. Jesus teaches His disciples to pray for their daily bread. This reminds us that prayer should be a daily practice and that we should rely on God for our daily needs.
4. Forgiveness is essential. In the Lord's Prayer, Jesus teaches His disciples to ask for forgiveness and to forgive others. Forgiveness is essential in our relationship with God and with others.

Conclusion: Jesus's teaching on prayer reminds us that prayer should be humble, focused on God's will, daily, and centered on forgiveness. May we learn from His teaching and make prayer a vital part of our daily lives, seeking to know God more deeply and aligning our lives with His will.

CHAPTER 15

The Word of God: What Jesus Says About the Scripture

JESUS HAS A high view of the Scripture and often refers to it in His teachings. In this chapter, we will explore what Jesus says about the Word of God.

What Jesus says about the Scripture:

1. The Scripture is authoritative: In Matthew 4:4, Jesus says, "It is written, 'Man shall not live by bread alone, but by every word that comes from the mouth of God.'" Jesus is quoting from Deuteronomy 8:3, showing that the Scripture is authoritative and essential for life.
2. The Scripture is true: In John 17:17, Jesus prays to the Father, saying, "Sanctify them in the truth; your word is truth." Jesus affirms that the Scripture is true and that it is the standard by which we should live our lives.
3. Scripture points to Jesus. In Luke 24:27, after His resurrection, Jesus appears to two disciples on the road to Emmaus, and "beginning with Moses and all the prophets, he interpreted to them in all the Scriptures the things concerning himself." Jesus shows that all of the Scripture points to Him as the Messiah.
4. The Scripture must be obeyed: In John 14:15, Jesus says, "If you love me, you will keep my commandments." Jesus's teachings in the Scripture are not just suggestions but commands that we must obey if we love Him.

What we can learn from Jesus's teaching:

1. We should study the Scripture. Jesus's high view of the Scripture should motivate us to study and understand it. Through the Scripture, we can know God more deeply and understand His will for our lives.
2. We should obey the Scripture. Jesus's teachings in the Scripture are not optional but essential for our lives. We should strive to obey His commands out of our love for Him.
3. The Scripture points to Jesus. All of the Scripture points to Jesus as the Messiah. We should read and study it with this in mind, seeking to know Him more deeply.

Conclusion: Jesus's teaching of the Scripture affirms its authority, truth, and importance for our lives. May we study and obey it, knowing that it points us to Jesus and the truth of God's will for our lives.

We read in 2 Timothy 3:16–17 (NIV), "All Scripture is God-breathed and is useful for teaching, rebuking, correcting and training in righteousness, so that the servant of God may be thoroughly equipped for every good work."

CHAPTER 16

The Lord's Supper: What Jesus Means by "Do This in Remembrance of Me"

IN THE GOSPELS, Jesus institutes the Lord's Supper, a meal of remembrance that Christians have continued to celebrate throughout the centuries. In this chapter, we will explore what Jesus means when he says, "Do this in remembrance of me."

What Jesus means by "Do This in Remembrance of Me": In Luke 22:19–20, Jesus takes bread, gives thanks, and breaks it, saying, "This is my body, which is given for you. Do this in remembrance of me." He then takes the cup and says, "This cup that is poured out for you is the new covenant in my blood."

1. Remembering Jesus's sacrifice: The Lord's Supper is a meal of remembrance, in which we remember Jesus's sacrifice on the cross for our sins. We remember that He gave His body and blood for us, and we give thanks for His love and grace.
2. Participating in the new covenant: Jesus's words about the cup being the new covenant in His blood remind us that we are participating in the new covenant through the Lord's Supper. The new covenant is the promise of salvation and eternal life through faith in Jesus Christ.

3. Communal eating: The Lord's Supper is a communal meal, in which we come together as the body of Christ to share in the bread and cup. We remember that we are part of a larger community of believers, and we are united in our faith in Jesus.

What we can learn from Jesus's teaching:

1. We should remember Jesus's sacrifice. The Lord's Supper is an opportunity for us to remember Jesus's sacrifice on the cross and to give thanks for His love and grace.
2. We should participate in the new covenant. Through the Lord's Supper, we participate in the new covenant that Jesus established through His death and resurrection.
3. We should come together as the body of Christ. The Lord's Supper is a communal meal, in which we come together as the body of Christ to share in the bread and cup and to remember our unity in faith.

Conclusion: Jesus's command to "do this in remembrance of me" is a call to remember His sacrifice, to participate in the new covenant, and to come together as the body of Christ. May we approach the Lord's Supper with gratitude and humility, remembering Jesus's love and grace for us.

When Jesus says, as often as you need to drink, do it a remembrance of me. I take this personally and realize for me that it means for every meal that I take in my personal life daily that I should remember Him and realize His presence and that His dying on the cross was for me, and for all of us. Remember, you asked for forgiveness of your sins first.

CHAPTER 17

Jesus's Teaching on Faith

FAITH IS A central concept in Christianity, and Jesus speaks frequently about it in His teachings. In this chapter, we will explore what Jesus says about faith.

Jesus's teaching on faith:

1. Faith can heal. Jesus often links faith with healing, telling people that their faith had made them well. For example, in Matthew 9:22, He says to a woman who had been bleeding for twelve years, "Take heart, daughter; your faith has made you well."
2. Faith is essential for salvation. In Mark 16:16, Jesus says, "Whoever believes and is baptized will be saved, but whoever does not believe will be condemned." Jesus teaches that faith in Him is necessary for salvation.
3. Faith can move mountains. In Matthew 17:20, Jesus tells His disciples, "Truly I tell you, if you have faith as small as a mustard seed, you can say to this mountain, 'Move from here to there,' and it will move. Nothing will be impossible for you." Jesus teaches that even a small amount of faith can have great power.
4. Faith requires trust: In John 14:1, Jesus says, "Do not let your hearts be troubled. You believe in God; believe also in me." Jesus teaches that faith requires trust in Him and in God.

What we can learn from Jesus's teaching:

1. Faith can bring healing. We should have faith that God can heal us, physically, emotionally, and spiritually.
2. Faith is essential for salvation. We must have faith in Jesus to be saved. Our faith should be in Him, and we should trust in His promises.
3. Faith can move mountains. Even a small amount of faith can have great power. We should trust in God's power to move mountains in our lives.
4. Faith requires trust. We should trust in God and in Jesus. We should not be afraid to put our faith in Him.

Conclusion: Jesus's teaching on faith reminds us that faith is essential for salvation, can bring healing, and can move mountains. May we have faith in God and in Jesus, trusting in Their promises and relying on their power in our lives.

CHAPTER 18

Jesus's Teaching on Anger

ANGER IS AN emotion that all humans experience, but it can also be harmful if not controlled. In his teachings, Jesus speaks about anger and how we can manage it in a healthy way. So let's explore what Jesus says about anger.

Jesus's teaching on anger:

1. Anger can lead to sin. In Matthew 5:21–22, Jesus says, "You have heard that it was said to those of ancient times, 'You shall not murder'; and 'whoever murders shall be liable to judgment.' But I say to you that if you are angry with a brother or sister, you will be liable to judgment." Jesus teaches that anger can lead to sin.
2. Reconciliation is important. In Matthew 5:23–24, Jesus says, "So when you are offering your gift at the altar, if you remember that your brother or sister has something against you, leave your gift there before the altar and go; first be reconciled to your brother or sister, and then come and offer your gift." Jesus teaches that reconciliation is important, even if it means setting aside our own pride.
3. Forgiveness is essential. In Matthew 18:21–22, Peter asks Jesus how many times he should forgive someone who has sinned against him. Jesus replies, "I do not say to you seven times, but seventy-seven times." Jesus teaches that forgiveness is essential, even if it means forgiving someone multiple times.

What we can learn from Jesus's teaching:

1. Anger can lead to sin. We should be careful not to let our anger control us. We should strive to manage our anger in a healthy way.
2. Reconciliation is important. We should seek reconciliation with others, even if it means setting aside our own pride. We should be willing to apologize and make amends.
3. Forgiveness is essential. We should forgive others, even if it means forgiving them multiple times. We should strive to let go of anger and bitterness and choose forgiveness instead.

Conclusion: Jesus's teaching on anger reminds us that anger can lead to sin and cause harm to ourselves and others. May we strive to manage our anger in a healthy way, seek reconciliation with others, and choose forgiveness over anger and bitterness. Remember, anger is just one letter short of danger.

CHAPTER 19

Jesus's Teaching on the Poor

JESUS HAS A heart for the poor and marginalized, and He often speaks about them in His teachings. In this chapter, we will explore what Jesus says about the poor.

Jesus's teaching on the poor:

1. The poor are blessed. In Luke 6:20, Jesus says, "Blessed are you who are poor, for yours is the kingdom of God." Jesus teaches that the poor are not forgotten by God and that they have a special place in His kingdom.
2. We should help the poor. In Matthew 25:35–36, Jesus says, "For I was hungry and you gave me food, I was thirsty and you gave me something to drink, I was a stranger and you welcomed me, I was naked and you gave me clothing, I was sick and you took care of me, I was in prison and you visited me." Jesus teaches that we should help the poor and marginalized and that when we do so, we are serving Him.
3. Wealth can be a barrier. In Mark 10:25, Jesus says, "It is easier for a camel to go through the eye of a needle than for someone who is rich to enter the kingdom of God." Jesus teaches that wealth can be a barrier to following Him and that it is important to prioritize our relationship with God over our earthly possessions.

What we can learn from Jesus's teaching:

1. The poor are blessed. We should remember that the poor are not forgotten by God and that they have a special place in His kingdom.
2. We should help the poor. We should strive to help the poor and marginalized in our communities, whether through acts of service, charitable giving, or advocacy.
3. Wealth can be a barrier. We should be careful not to prioritize our earthly possessions over our relationship with God. We should strive to live simply and generously, following Jesus's example.

Conclusion: Jesus's teaching of the poor reminds us of the importance of caring for the marginalized and vulnerable in our communities. May we have a heart for the poor, strive to help them in tangible ways, and prioritize our relationship with God over our earthly possessions.

In my own personal life, I understand what poor is, and I've seen so much poverty throughout my entire career in law enforcement. I've learned that I'm not moved by what I see but by what is in the hearts and minds of the people. The worst of being poor is to be poor in spirit. Once Jesus enters our life, then the material things in our life are not as important.

Here is a very important verse in my life: "He who is gracious and lends a hand to the poor lends to the Lord, And the Lord will repay him for his good deed" (Prov. 19:17, AMP).

CHAPTER 20

Jesus's Teaching on Children

CHILDREN ARE IMPORTANT to Jesus, and he often uses them as an example in his teachings. In this chapter, we will explore what Jesus says about children.

Jesus's teaching on children:

1. Children are important. In Matthew 19:14, Jesus says, "Let the little children come to me, and do not stop them; for it is to such as these that the kingdom of heaven belongs." Jesus teaches that children are important and have a special place in his kingdom.
2. We should have childlike faith. In Matthew 18:3–4, Jesus says, "Truly I tell you, unless you change and become like children, you will never enter the kingdom of heaven. Whoever becomes humble like this child is the greatest in the kingdom of heaven." Jesus teaches that we should have childlike faith, characterized by humility and trust in God.
3. We should protect children. In Matthew 18:6, Jesus says, "If any of you put a stumbling block before one of these little ones who believe in me, it would be better for you if a great millstone were fastened around your neck and you were drowned in the depth of the sea." Jesus teaches that we should protect children and not lead them astray.

What we can learn from Jesus's teaching:

1. Children are important. We should value and care for the children in our lives, recognizing their importance in God's kingdom.
2. We should have childlike faith. We should strive to have a humble and trusting faith like that of a child, recognizing our need for God and His grace.
3. We should protect children. We should be mindful of the impact our words and actions can have on children and strive to protect them from harm.

Conclusion: Jesus's teaching about children reminds us of their importance and value in God's kingdom. May we strive to have childlike faith, care for, and protect the children in our lives, and recognize their unique place in God's plan.

We have an obligation to take care of our children. Here is some additional information about what is occurring in our society today that I'll share with a story:

Once upon a time, there was a small town where the people lived in peace and harmony. However, behind closed doors, some children were suffering from abuse and neglect. As the years went by, the problem of child abuse became more prevalent, and the town was no longer the peaceful place it once was.

According to statistical data from the National Children's Alliance, an estimated 1,770 children die from abuse and neglect in the United States each year. This means that on average, four children die every day due to child abuse. Furthermore, the National Children's Alliance reports that in 2019, over six hundred thousand children were victims of abuse or neglect in the United States alone.

In this small town, the statistics were just as alarming. According to the local child protective services agency, there were fifty confirmed cases of child abuse and neglect in the town in the past year. This was a 25 percent increase from the previous year, and it was clear that something had to be done.

Fortunately, the town came together to address the issue of child abuse. Community leaders, law enforcement officials, and concerned citizens formed a task force to raise awareness about the problem and provide support to victims and their families. They organized town hall meetings, distributed educational materials, and worked with local schools to identify and report signs of abuse.

Through the hard work of the task force, the people of the town began to understand that child abuse was a serious problem that affected everyone. They learned that child abuse could have lifelong consequences for victims, including mental health issues, substance abuse, and even death. They also learned that by coming together as a community, they could make a difference in the lives of these children.

As the years went by, the town saw a significant decrease in the number of child abuse cases, and it became a safer and more peaceful place for children to grow up. The statistics continued to improve, and the town was proud of the progress it had made in protecting its most vulnerable citizens.

The story of this small town serves as a reminder that child abuse is a serious problem that affects children of all ages, races, and socioeconomic backgrounds. It also shows that by working together as a community, we can make a difference in the lives of these children and help them heal from the trauma of abuse.

Let us become more mindful, prayerful, and active in preventing and protecting our children. When a community pulls together, we can accomplish much. I like the City of Fort Collins, Colorado statement: "Together we are better."

References

Child Welfare Information Gateway. 2020. Child Abuse and Neglect

Statistics. https://www.childwelfare.gov/pubPDFs/canstats.pdf

National Children's Alliance. 2020. Child Abuse Statistics &

Facts. https://www.nationalchildrensalliance.org/media-room/media-kit/child-abuse-statistics-facts/

CHAPTER 21

Jesus's Teaching on Orphans

ORPHANS ARE AMONG the most vulnerable in Jesus's time, and He has a heart for them. We will explore what Jesus says about orphans.

Jesus's teaching on orphans:

1. God cares for orphans: In John 14:18, Jesus says, "I will not leave you orphaned; I am coming to you." Jesus teaches that God cares for orphans and will not leave them alone.
2. We should care for orphans. James 1:27 says, "Religion that is pure and undefiled before God, the Father, is this: to care for orphans and widows in their distress." Jesus teaches that caring for orphans is an important part of living out our faith.
3. We should welcome orphans. In Matthew 25:40, Jesus says, "Truly I tell you, just as you did it to one of the least of these who are members of my family, you did it to me." Jesus teaches that when we welcome and care for orphans, we are caring for Him.

What we can learn from Jesus's teaching:

1. God cares for orphans. We should remember that God cares for orphans and is present with them, even in their most difficult moments.

2. We should care for orphans. We should strive to care for orphans in our communities, whether through adoption, fostering, or supporting organizations that serve them.
3. We should welcome orphans. We should welcome and love orphans as we would welcome and love Jesus himself, recognizing their inherent worth and value.

Conclusion: Jesus's teaching about orphans reminds us of their vulnerability and the importance of caring for them. May we have a heart for orphans, strive to care for and welcome them into our communities, and recognize their value as beloved children of God.

I was raised in the orphanage until age five when my adoptive parents brought me home to Fort Collins and claimed me as their own. There is a huge difference between living in the Colorado State Orphanage for Neglected and Dependent Children and living in your own room with a closet. God made room for me because He had a plan.

According to the Adoption and Foster Care Analysis and Reporting System (AFCARS), as of 2020, there were approximately 424,000 children in foster care in the United States. It is important to note that not all children in foster care live in orphanages; they may also live with foster families or in group homes. Although it is difficult to quantify, roughly 20,000 children "age out" of foster care each year. This means they are now legally adults without ever finding a family through adoption. That alone saddens me. Everyone wants to identify with a family.

Reference

The Healthy Journal. n.d. *Frequently Asked Questions*. https://www.thehealthyjournal.com/frequently-asked-questions/how-many-newborns-go-unadopted-in-the-us#:~:text=Although%20it%20is%20difficult%20to,finding%20a%20family%20through%20adoption

CHAPTER 22

Jesus's Authority Over Demons

THROUGHOUT JESUS'S MINISTRY, he encounters many people who are possessed by demons. In this chapter, we will explore what Jesus does about the demons.

Jesus's authority over demons:

1. Jesus casts out demons. Mark 1:34 says, "And he cured many who were sick with various diseases, and cast out many demons." Jesus has the power and authority to cast out demons and heal those who were possessed.
2. Jesus's authority is recognized. In Mark 5:7, a demon-possessed man says to Jesus, "What have you to do with me, Jesus, Son of the Most High God? I adjure you by God, do not torment me." The demons recognize Jesus's authority and power over them.
3. Demons are subject to Jesus. Luke 10:17 says, "The seventy returned with joy, saying, 'Lord, in your name even the demons submit to us!'" Jesus's disciples are able to cast out demons in His name, demonstrating the power and authority that Jesus has over them.

What we can learn from Jesus's authority over demons:

1. Jesus has power over evil. We should remember that Jesus has power and authority over evil, including demons.

2. Jesus's authority is recognized. We should recognize Jesus's authority and power over evil, and submit to Him as our Lord and Savior.
3. Jesus's power is available to us: We can have access to the power and authority of Jesus through prayer and faith, and can overcome evil in our lives through His name.

Conclusion: Jesus's authority over demons demonstrates His power and authority over all evil. May we trust in His power and authority and call on Him to help us overcome evil in our lives.

CHAPTER 23

Exercising Jesus's Power

AS FOLLOWERS OF Jesus, we are called to exercise the power and authority He has given us. Join me in learning how Jesus teaches us to exercise His power.

Exercising Jesus's power:

1. Through prayer: In Matthew 21:21–22, Jesus says, "Truly I tell you, if you have faith and do not doubt, not only will you do what has been done to the fig tree, but even if you say to this mountain, 'Be lifted up and thrown into the sea,' it will be done. Whatever you ask for in prayer with faith, you will receive." Jesus teaches that we can exercise His power through prayer and faith.
2. With humility: In Matthew 20:26–28, Jesus says, "Whoever wishes to be great among you must be your servant, and whoever wishes to be first among you must be your slave; just as the Son of Man came not to be served but to serve." Jesus teaches that we should exercise His power with humility, serving others and putting their needs before our own.
3. Through obedience: In John 14:15, Jesus says, "If you love me, you will keep my commandments." Jesus teaches that we can exercise His power through obedience to His teachings and commands.

What we can learn from Jesus's teaching:

1. Power through prayer: We should exercise Jesus's power through prayer, asking for His help and guidance in all areas of our lives.
2. Power with humility: We should exercise Jesus's power with humility, serving others and putting their needs before our own.
3. Power through obedience: We should exercise Jesus's power through obedience to his teachings and commands, living our lives in a way that honors Him.

Conclusion: Jesus's teaching on exercising His power reminds us that we have access to His power and authority as we seek to follow Him. May we exercise His power through prayer, humility, and obedience, trusting in His guidance and strength in all that we do.

CHAPTER 24

The Power of Saying "In the Name of Jesus"

IN CHRISTIANITY, SAYING "in the name of Jesus" is a common practice used in prayer and spiritual activities. This phrase is not just a set of words, but a declaration of faith and dependence on Jesus's power and authority. In this chapter, we will explore why we are taught to say "in the name of Jesus" and the power it holds.

The authority of Jesus: One reason why we are taught to say "in the name of Jesus" is because of His authority. Christians believe that Jesus is the Son of God and has ultimate power and authority over all things. In Matthew 28:18, Jesus says, "All authority in heaven and on earth has been given to me." By saying "in the name of Jesus," we are invoking His authority and acknowledging that He has the power to act on our behalf.

Biblical precedent: Another reason why we are taught to say "in the name of Jesus" is because of the biblical precedent. In the New Testament, Jesus's followers often used His name to perform miracles and healing. For example, in Acts 3:6, Peter says to a lame beggar, "In the name of Jesus Christ of Nazareth, walk." The beggar is healed and begins to walk. Christians believe that using Jesus's name is a powerful tool for performing miracles and healing.

Expression of faith: Saying "in the name of Jesus" is also an expression of faith in His power and authority. By using His name, Christians are declaring their belief that He can act on their behalf and accomplish their prayers or actions. In John 14:13–14, Jesus says, "Whatever you ask in my name, I will do it, so that the Father may be glorified in the Son. If in my name you ask me for anything, I will do it." By saying "in the name of Jesus," we are expressing our faith that He will act on our behalf.

Protection against evil: Finally, saying "in the name of Jesus" is also a way of protecting ourselves against evil. Christians believe that there is power in Jesus's name to overcome evil forces. Luke 10:17 says, "The seventy returned with joy, saying, 'Lord, in your name even the demons submit to us!'" By using His name, we are declaring our allegiance to Jesus and seeking His protection against the forces of darkness.

Conclusion: Saying "in the name of Jesus" is a declaration of faith and dependence on His power and authority. It is a way of acknowledging His role as Savior and Lord and expressing our faith in Him. By using His name, we are invoking His authority, following the biblical precedent, expressing our faith, and seeking His protection against evil. May we always remember the power of saying "in the name of Jesus" and use it to honor Him in all that we do.

CHAPTER 25

The Role of Women in Jesus's Ministry

JESUS CHRIST IS often revered as a revolutionary figure in His approach toward women. He challenged the patriarchal norms of His time and elevated the status of women in society. In this chapter, we will explore what Jesus says about women and their role in His ministry.

The woman at the well: One of the most notable encounters Jesus has with a woman is recorded in John 4:1–42. Jesus meets a Samaritan woman at a well and engages in a conversation with her, despite the cultural and religious boundaries that exist between them. He offers her living water, which symbolizes eternal life, and reveals that He is the Messiah. The woman becomes a witness to her community, and many Samaritans come to believe in Jesus. This encounter shows that Jesus sees women as valuable and worthy of His time and attention.

The woman caught in adultery: In John 8:1–11, Jesus encounters a woman who is caught in the act of adultery. The religious leaders bring her to him, intending to stone her, but Jesus challenges them to examine their own sinfulness. He then tells the woman, "Neither do I condemn you; go, and from now on sin no more." This interaction reveals Jesus's mercy and compassion toward women who are often shamed and condemned for their actions.

Mary and Martha: In Luke 10:38–42, Jesus visits the home of two sisters, Mary and Martha. While Martha is busy preparing food, Mary sits at Jesus's feet and listens to his teachings. Martha becomes frustrated with her sister and asks Jesus to tell her to help. Jesus responds, "Martha, Martha, you are worried and distracted by many things; there is need of only one thing. Mary has chosen the better part, which will not be taken away from her." Jesus's response highlights the importance of women's spiritual development and their ability to learn from His teachings.

The women at the cross: At the crucifixion, women are among the few who remain with Jesus until the end. In John 19:25–27, Jesus entrusts the care of his mother to the disciple whom he loves, believed to be John. This act shows Jesus's concern for the well-being of women and their importance in His life.

Conclusion: Jesus's interactions with women reveal His compassion, mercy, and respect for them. He challenges the patriarchal norms of His time and elevates the status of women in society. Women play an important role in His ministry, from being His disciples to being witnesses of His resurrection. May we learn from Jesus's example and continue to recognize the value and worth of women in our society.

One woman in the Bible who is a leader and prophetess is Deborah. She lives during a time when Israel is oppressed by the Canaanites, and she serves as a judge and ruler over Israel. She is known for her wisdom and her ability to hear from God. Deborah is a strong and courageous leader, and she leads the Israelites to victory against their oppressors.

Another woman in the Bible who spreads the word of God is Mary Magdalene. She is one of the disciples of Jesus and is present at His crucifixion and resurrection. After His resurrection, Jesus appears to Mary first and instructs her to go and tell the other disciples that He has risen. Mary is a faithful disciple and spread the word of Jesus's resurrection to others.

Another woman in the Bible who is a prophetess was Huldah. She lives during the reign of King Josiah, and when a copy of the Book of the Law is found in the temple, it is brought to Huldah for interpretation. She confirms that the book is indeed from God and warns the people that judgment would come upon them if they do not repent.

These women, among others, play important roles in spreading the word of God and leading God's people. Their stories serve as inspiration for women today to use their gifts and talents to serve God and lead others in His ways.

CHAPTER 26

The Importance of Compassion in Jesus's Teaching

INTRODUCTION: COMPASSION IS a fundamental aspect of Jesus's teaching. He emphasizes the importance of showing love and kindness towards others, especially those who are marginalized and vulnerable. In this chapter, we will explore what Jesus says about compassion and its significance in our lives.

The good Samaritan: In Luke 10:25–37, Jesus tells the parable of the good Samaritan. A man is beaten and left for dead on the side of the road. A priest and a Levite pass by without helping him, but a Samaritan, who is despised by Jews, stops to care for him. The Samaritan bandages the man's wounds, takes him to an inn, and pays for his care. Jesus teaches that we should love our neighbors as ourselves, even if they are from a different race or religion. The good Samaritan demonstrates compassion toward the injured man, despite the social and cultural barriers that exist between them.

The prodigal son: In Luke 15:11–32, Jesus tells the parable of the prodigal son. A young man asks his father for his inheritance early and squanders it on wild living. He eventually becomes destitute and returns home, hoping to be a servant in his father's house. But the father welcomes him back with open arms and celebrates his return. The older brother becomes angry and jealous, but the father reminds him that they should be happy that the lost son has been found. This parable shows that God is compassionate and forgiving, even toward those who have made mistakes and rebelled against Him.

The Beatitudes: In Matthew 5:3–12, Jesus teaches the Beatitudes, a series of blessings for those who are humble, merciful, and peacemakers. He teaches that those who mourn will be comforted, the meek will inherit the earth, and the merciful will receive mercy. The Beatitudes promote compassion and kindness toward others, as well as a focus on spiritual growth and humility.

The last judgment: In Matthew 25:31–46, Jesus teaches about the last judgment, where the Son of Man separates the sheep from the goats. The sheep are those who have shown compassion toward others, feeding the hungry, clothing the naked, and visiting the sick and imprisoned. The goats are those who have not shown compassion toward others. Jesus teaches that whatever we do for the least of these, we do for Him. This passage emphasizes the importance of showing compassion toward others, especially those who are in need.

Conclusion: Compassion is a central aspect of Jesus's teaching. He teaches that we should love our neighbors as ourselves, even if they are different from us. He emphasizes forgiveness and mercy toward those who have made mistakes and encouraged us to focus on spiritual growth and humility. May we follow Jesus's example and strive to show compassion towards others in our daily lives.

I remember when the soccer team boys in Thailand were stuck in a cave because of the flooding water. There was a cry around the world to see what we could do to rescue them. The only thing I could do was constantly pray for them every day. My heart was moved with so much compassion for them that I found myself in tears every day praying for their recovery.

Everyone was saved. Not because of me, but because of the prayers of so many people around the world. People were moved with compassion, regardless of the religion that the Thai boys and their coach were following.

Here are some interesting references and studies that were done. Compassion is a powerful emotion that is linked to numerous physical and mental health benefits. Here are some references that support the health benefits of compassion:

1. Reduced inflammation: A study published in *Psychoneuroendocrinology* found that participants who practiced compassion meditation had lower levels of inflammatory markers in their blood compared to those who did not practice compassion meditation.
2. Improved cardiovascular health: A study published in the *Journal of Behavioral Medicine* found that individuals who reported higher levels of compassion had lower levels of stress and better cardiovascular health.
3. Enhanced immune function: A study published in the *Annals of Behavioral Medicine* found that individuals who practiced loving-kindness meditation, a type of meditation that cultivates compassion, had enhanced immune function.
4. Reduced depression and anxiety: A study published in the *Journal of Consulting and Clinical Psychology* found that compassion-focused therapy was effective in reducing symptoms of depression and anxiety in participants.
5. Increased life satisfaction: A study published in the *Journal of Happiness Studies* found that individuals who practiced compassion had higher levels of life satisfaction.

Overall, these studies suggest that practicing compassion can have a positive impact on both physical and mental health. It can reduce inflammation, improve cardiovascular health, enhance immune function, reduce depression and anxiety, and increase life satisfaction.

CHAPTER 27

The Power of Silence in Jesus's Ministry

JESUS IS OFTEN questioned by the religious leaders of his time, who seek to trap him in His words. However, Jesus chooses to remain silent at times, much to the confusion of those around him. In this chapter, we will explore why Jesus chooses to be silent when questioned and what we can learn from His example.

Silence in the face of accusations: In Matthew 26:57–68, Jesus is brought before the high priest, who questions Him about His teachings. The high priest accuses Jesus of blasphemy and demands that He answer. However, Jesus remains silent. His silence is significant because it shows that He was not intimidated by the accusations and did not feel the need to defend Himself or His teachings.

Silence as a form of witness: In Mark 14:60–62, Jesus is questioned by the high priest again. This time, the high priest asks Jesus directly if He is the Messiah. Jesus responds, "I am, and you will see the Son of Man seated at the right hand of power and coming with the clouds of heaven." Jesus's response is significant because He is essentially claiming to be the Son of God, which is a capital offense at the time. Jesus's response is also significant because he chooses to speak rather than remain silent. This shows that Jesus is not afraid to speak truth to power, even if it means risking His life.

Silence in the face of mockery: In Matthew 27:11–14, Jesus is brought before Pilate, the Roman governor. Pilate questions Jesus about His kingship and asks if He is the King of the Jews. Jesus responds, "You say so." Pilate is confused by Jesus's response and asks Him why He is not defending Himself against the accusations of the religious leaders. Jesus remains silent. His silence is significant because it shows that He is not interested in engaging in meaningless arguments or defending Himself against false accusations.

Conclusion: Jesus's use of silence in His ministry is a powerful tool that allows Him to remain focused on His mission and speak truth to power. His silence in the face of accusations and mockery shows that He is not intimidated by those who seek to trap him in His words. His willingness to speak truth to power, even if it means risking His life, shows that He is committed to His message of love and compassion. May we learn from Jesus's example and use silence as a tool to remain focused on our mission and speak truth to power in our daily lives.

Consider this verse and pause and meditate on it: "Be still, and know that I am God" (Ps. 46:10, KJV).

CHAPTER 27

The Significance of Fasting in Jesus's Teaching

INTRODUCTION: FASTING IS a spiritual discipline that has been practiced by many religions throughout history. In Christianity, fasting is often seen as a way to deepen one's relationship with God and focus on spiritual growth. In this chapter, we will explore what Jesus says about fasting and its significance in His teaching.

The purpose of fasting: In Matthew 6:16–18, Jesus teaches about fasting. He says, "When you fast, do not look gloomy like the hypocrites, for they disfigure their faces that their fasting may be seen by others. Truly, I say to you, they have received their reward. But when you fast, anoint your head and wash your face, that your fasting may not be seen by others but by your Father who is in secret. And your Father who sees in secret will reward you." Jesus emphasizes that fasting should not be done for show or to gain the approval of others. Instead, fasting is a personal discipline that should be done with humility and sincerity.

The benefits of fasting: In Matthew 17:14–21, Jesus casts out a demon from a boy who is suffering from seizures. The disciples try to cast out the demon but were unsuccessful. When they ask Jesus why they couldn't do it, he replies, "This kind cannot be driven out by anything but prayer and fasting." Jesus's response indicates that fasting can be a powerful tool in spiritual warfare and can help us to overcome spiritual obstacles.

The attitude of fasting: In Luke 18:9–14, Jesus tells the parable of the Pharisee and the tax collector. The Pharisee fasts twice a week and boasts about his righteousness, while the tax collector humbly asks for God's mercy. Jesus uses this parable to teach about the attitude of fasting. Fasting should not be done for self-righteousness or to gain the approval of others. Instead, it should be done with humility and a desire to draw closer to God.

Conclusion: Fasting is a spiritual discipline that can help us to deepen our relationship with God and focus on spiritual growth. Jesus emphasizes that fasting should be done with humility and sincerity, not for show or self-righteousness. He also teaches that fasting can be a powerful tool in spiritual warfare and can help us to overcome spiritual obstacles. May we follow Jesus's example and practice fasting with humility, sincerity, and a desire to draw closer to God.

I have found that fasting not only draws me closer to God, but fasting creates a sense of humbleness, a hunger to learn and know more, a sense of intuitiveness, a feeling of forgiveness not only for myself but for others, and a closer bond with God. When all these characteristics are combined, somehow, I derive answers from Him, and I hear a voice of reasoning from God.

CHAPTER 28

The Passion of Christ: A Reflection on Jesus's Suffering

THE PASSION OF Christ refers to the events leading up to Jesus's crucifixion and His subsequent death on the cross. The passion of Christ is a central theme in Christian theology, and it serves as a reminder of Jesus's sacrifice and love for humanity. In this chapter, we will reflect on Jesus's passion and what it reveals about His character and His mission.

Agony in the garden: In Matthew 26:36–46, Jesus goes to the Garden of Gethsemane to pray before his arrest. He is overwhelmed with sorrow and asks His disciples to stay with him and pray. Jesus's agony in the Garden reveals His humanity and His willingness to suffer for the sake of others. Despite knowing what lay ahead, Jesus remains steadfast in His mission and committed to fulfilling God's plan.

The betrayal: In Matthew 26:47–56, Jesus is betrayed by Judas and arrested by the Roman soldiers. Jesus's betrayal by one of His closest disciples reveals the depth of human sin and the extent of Jesus's love and forgiveness. Even in the face of betrayal, Jesus remains committed to His mission and does not retaliate against His enemies.

The trial: In Matthew 26:57–68 and Matthew 27:11–26, Jesus is brought before the Jewish leaders and the Roman governor, Pontius Pilate, for trial. He is accused of blasphemy and sedition, and He is ultimately sentenced to death by crucifixion. Jesus's trial reveals the injustice and corruption of human institutions and the extent to which power can corrupt. Despite being falsely accused and unjustly sentenced, Jesus remains committed to His mission and did not back down from His teachings.

The crucifixion: In Matthew 27:32–50, Jesus is crucified on the cross. He suffers intense physical pain and is mocked by the onlookers. Jesus's crucifixion reveals the depth of His love for humanity and His willingness to suffer for the sake of others. Even in His final moments, Jesus forgives His enemies and entrusts His spirit to God.

Conclusion: The passion of Christ is a reminder of Jesus's sacrifice and love for humanity. His agony in the garden and the betrayal, trial, and crucifixion reveal the depth of His character and his commitment to His mission. Let's reflect on Jesus's passion and be inspired to follow His example of love, forgiveness, and sacrifice in our own lives.

CHAPTER 29

Understanding Fear According to Jesus

FEAR IS A natural human emotion that can be caused by various factors, including perceived danger, uncertainty, or the unknown. In this chapter, we will explore what Jesus says about fear, its effects on our lives, and how we can overcome it.

The nature of fear: According to Jesus, fear is a common human emotion that can manifest in many different ways. In Matthew 10:28, He says, "Do not be afraid of those who kill the body but cannot kill the soul. Rather, be afraid of the one who can destroy both soul and body in hell." Jesus acknowledges that there are real threats and dangers in the world, but He urges His followers to trust in God and not be consumed by fear.

The effects of fear: Jesus warns that fear can have negative effects on our lives, both physically and spiritually. In Matthew 14:31, He says to Peter, who was walking on water with Him, "You of little faith," He says, "Why did you doubt?" Jesus points out that fear can prevent us from fully trusting in God and can lead to doubt and a lack of faith.

Overcoming fear: Jesus offers several strategies for overcoming fear and anxiety. In John 14:27, He says, "Peace I leave with you; my peace I give you. I do not give to you as the world gives. Do not let your hearts be troubled and do not be afraid." Jesus encourages His followers to seek His peace and trust in His presence, rather than being consumed by fear.

The power of faith: Jesus emphasizes the importance of faith in overcoming fear. In Matthew 17:20, He says, "Truly I tell you, if you have faith as small as a mustard seed, you can say to this mountain, 'Move from here to there,' and it will move. Nothing will be impossible for you." Jesus urges His followers to have faith in God's power and presence, rather than being consumed by fear.

Trusting in God: Finally, Jesus encourages His followers to trust in God's provision and care, even in the face of fear. In Matthew 6:25–26, He says, "Therefore I tell you, do not worry about your life, what you will eat or drink; or about your body, what you will wear. Is not life more than food, and the body more than clothes? Look at the birds of the air; they do not sow or reap or store away in barns, and yet your heavenly Father feeds them. Are you not much more valuable than they?" Jesus reminds us that we are valuable to God and that we can trust in His care and provision, even in uncertain or fearful situations.

In conclusion, Jesus speaks of fear as a common human emotion that can be overcome through faith in God and trust in His provision and care. He warns of the negative effects of fear on our lives and offered strategies for overcoming it, including seeking His peace, having faith, and trusting in God's care.

Fear is mentioned 365 times in the Bible, so it's kind of a big deal and we should deal with it.

I've prepared a poem that is fitting for this chapter:

Fear grips me tight with icy fingers,
A chill that lingers and never lingers,
It whispers lies and makes me weak,
My heart races, my knees grow weak.

It tells me stories of what could be,
Of all the dangers I cannot see,
It paralyzes, it steals my joy,
It makes me feel like just a toy.

But then a voice, soft and strong,
Whispers gently, "You belong,
To me, my child, you are loved,
And by my side, you are unshoved."

With that assurance in my heart,
I take a deep breath, make a start,
To face my fears with courage bold,
And trust in the One who never grows old.

For fear may come and fear may go,
But with my Savior, I will grow,
In strength and faith, in hope and love,
Till fear is just a memory of.

So let fear come, let fear go,
For with my Savior, I will grow,
In courage and in steadfast trust,
Till fear is just a fleeting gust.

CHAPTER 30

Understanding Worry According to Jesus

JESUS SPEAKS OFTEN about the dangers of worry, describing it as a hindrance to our spiritual growth and a sign of a lack of faith. In this chapter, we will explore what Jesus says about worry, its effects on our lives, and how we can overcome it.

The nature of worry: According to Jesus, worry is a form of anxiety or fear about the future. In Matthew 6:25, He says, "Therefore I tell you, do not worry about your life, what you will eat or drink; or about your body, what you will wear. Is not life more than food, and the body more than clothes?" Jesus acknowledges that worry is a natural human response to the uncertainties of life, but he urges his followers to trust in God instead of worrying.

The effects of worry: Jesus warns that worry can have negative effects on our lives, both physically and spiritually. In Matthew 6:27, He says, "Can any one of you by worrying add a single hour to your life?" He also says in Matthew 6:33, "But seek first his kingdom and his righteousness, and all these things will be given to you as well." Jesus points out that worry can distract us from what is truly important in life and prevent us from living fully in the present moment.

Overcoming worry: Jesus offers several strategies for overcoming worry and anxiety. In Matthew 6:31–32, he says, "So do not worry, saying, 'What shall we eat?' or 'What shall we drink?' or 'What shall we wear?' For the pagans run after all these things, and your heavenly Father knows that you need them." Jesus encourages his followers to trust in God's provision, rather than worrying about material possessions or the future.

The power of faith: Jesus emphasizes the importance of faith in overcoming worry. In Matthew 6:30, He says, "If that is how God clothes the grass of the field, which is here today and tomorrow is thrown into the fire, will he not much more clothe you—you of little faith?" Jesus urges His followers to have faith in God's provision and care, rather than worrying about their basic needs.

Living in the present moment: Finally, Jesus encourages His followers to live in the present moment and not worry about the future. In Matthew 6:34, He says, "Therefore do not worry about tomorrow, for tomorrow will worry about itself. Each day has enough trouble of its own." Jesus reminds us that worrying about the future only adds unnecessary stress to our lives and can prevent us from fully enjoying the present moment.

In conclusion, Jesus speaks of worry as a hindrance to our spiritual growth and a sign of a lack of faith. He warns of the negative effects of worry on our lives and offers strategies for overcoming it, including trusting in God's provision and care, having faith, and living in the present moment.

This is such an important topic. I've provided you with more information about medical research that may help you identify why you are experiencing some symptoms. Worrying is a natural human response to events or situations that we perceive as threatening or stressful. Excessive worrying can have negative effects on our physical and mental health. Let's explore the ways in which worrying can cause physical and mental ailments and consider strategies for managing worry and anxiety.

Physical ailments. Excessive worrying can lead to a range of physical ailments, including:

1. Digestive problems: Worrying can cause digestive problems such as stomach pain, bloating, diarrhea, and constipation. This is because worry can trigger the release of stress hormones such as cortisol, which can affect the digestive system.
2. Headaches: Chronic worrying can cause tension headaches, which are characterized by a tight band-like sensation around the head.
3. Cardiovascular problems: Studies have shown that worrying can lead to an increased risk of cardiovascular problems such as high blood pressure, heart disease, and stroke. This is because stress hormones can cause inflammation in the blood vessels, which can lead to the narrowing and hardening of the arteries.

Mental Ailments. Excessive worrying can also lead to a range of mental health problems, including:

1. Anxiety disorders: Chronic worrying can lead to anxiety disorders such as generalized anxiety disorder (GAD), panic disorder, and obsessive-compulsive disorder (OCD). These disorders are characterized by persistent and excessive worry that can interfere with daily life.
2. Depression: Worrying can also lead to depression, which is characterized by feelings of sadness, hopelessness, and a loss of interest in activities that were once enjoyable.
3. Insomnia: Worrying can make it difficult to fall asleep or stay asleep, leading to insomnia. This can cause fatigue, irritability, and difficulty concentrating during the day.

References

American Heart Association. 2019. *Stress and heart health*. Retrieved from https://www.heart.org/en/healthy-living/healthy-lifestyle/stress-management/stress-and-heart-health

Harvard Health Publishing. 2018. *The gut-brain connection*. Retrieved from https://www.health.harvard.edu/diseases-and-conditions/the-gut-brain-connection

Mayo Clinic. 2019. *Chronic stress puts your health at risk*. Retrieved from https://www.mayoclinic.org/healthy-lifestyle/stress-management/in-depth/stress/art-20046037

National Institute of Mental Health. 2018. *Anxiety disorders*. Retrieved from https://www.nimh.nih.gov/health/topics/anxiety-disorders/index.shtml

National Institute of Mental Health. 2018. *Depression*. Retrieved from https://www.nimh.nih.gov/health/topics/depression/index.shtml

National Sleep Foundation. n.d. *Insomnia*. Retrieved from https://www.sleepfoundation.org/insomnia

CHAPTER 31

Understanding Angels According to Jesus

JESUS SPOKE OFTEN about angels, describing them as heavenly beings who carry out the will of God. In this chapter, we will explore what Jesus says about angels and their role in the spiritual realm.

The nature of angels: According to Jesus, angels are spiritual beings who serve God in the heavenly realm. In Matthew 22:30, Jesus says that in the resurrection, people will be like angels in heaven who do not marry or give in marriage. In Luke 20:35–36, He says that those who are considered worthy of the resurrection will be like angels and will not die.

The role of angels: Jesus speaks of angels as messengers and servants of God. In Matthew 24:31, He says that the angels will gather His elect from the four winds, from one end of heaven to the other. In Luke 16:22, He describes the death of the rich man and the beggar, with the beggar being carried by angels to Abraham's side.

Angels and spiritual warfare: Jesus also speaks of angels as warriors in the spiritual realm. In Matthew 13:41–42, He describes the angels as separating the wicked from the righteous and throwing them into the fiery furnace. In Revelation 12:7–9, He describes a war in heaven between the dragon (Satan) and the angels of God.

The relationship between angels and humans: Jesus speaks of angels as having a special concern for human beings. In Luke

15:10, He says that there is rejoicing in the presence of the angels of God over one sinner who repents. In Matthew 18:10, He says that the angels of children always see the face of God. In Hebrews 1:14, the author speaks of angels as ministering spirits sent out to serve the sake of those who are to inherit salvation.

The role of Jesus and angels: Finally, Jesus speaks of His own relationship with the angels. In Matthew 26:53, He tells Peter that He could call on His Father and He would send more than twelve legions of angels to His defense. In Luke 22:43, an angel appears to Jesus in the Garden of Gethsemane to strengthen Him.

The book of Luke mentions an angel who appeared to Jesus in the Garden of Gethsemane to strengthen Him. The Bible does not give us a physical description of the appearance of the angel in this instance. However, the angel is sent to provide comfort and support to Jesus during his time of distress. The appearance of angels in the Bible is often described as awe-inspiring and powerful, with bright light, wings, and a majestic presence. However, it is important to remember that the appearance of angels can vary depending on the purpose for which they are sent and that their true nature as spiritual beings may be beyond human comprehension.

In conclusion, Jesus speaks of angels as spiritual beings who serve God in the heavenly realm, carrying out His will and ministering to human beings. He also speaks of their role in spiritual warfare and their relationship with Him as the Son of God.

Angels are very real in my life. I intend to write another book about my experiences with angels and about dreams.

CHAPTER 32

Understanding Hell According to Jesus

JESUS SPEAKS OFTEN about the reality of hell, describing it as a place of eternal punishment and separation from God. In Matthew 25:41, Jesus says that those who do not follow Him will be sent to "the eternal fire prepared for the devil and his angels." In this chapter, we will explore what Jesus says about hell and its implications for our lives.

The nature of hell: According to Jesus, hell is a place of eternal punishment and torment. In Matthew 25:46, Jesus says that the punishment of the wicked is "eternal punishment." In Mark 9:48, He describes hell as a place where "their worm does not die and the fire is not quenched." Jesus also speaks of hell as a place of darkness and separation from God (Matt. 8:12, 22:13).

Who goes to hell? Jesus makes it clear that those who reject Him, and His message will be sent to hell. In Matthew 7:13–14, he says that the way to eternal life is narrow, and few will find it, while the way to destruction is wide and many will enter it. In Matthew 25:41, he says that those who do not follow him will be sent to "the eternal fire prepared for the devil and his angels."

The urgency of repentance: Jesus urges His listeners to repent and turn to God in order to avoid the punishment of hell. In Luke 13:3, He says, "Unless you repent, you will all likewise perish." In Matthew 4:17, He begins his ministry by saying, "Repent, for the kingdom of heaven is at hand." Jesus also tells the story of the rich man and Lazarus, in which the rich man begs Abraham to send Lazarus to warn his brothers to repent so that they will not end up in the place of torment (Luke 16:19–31).

The role of judgment: Jesus speaks of a final judgment in which all people will be judged according to their deeds. In Matthew 25:31–46, He describes the separation of the sheep and the goats, with the sheep being rewarded with eternal life and the goats being sent to eternal punishment. In John 5:28–29, He says that all who are in the tombs will hear his voice and come out, those who have done good to the resurrection of life, and those who have done evil to the resurrection of judgment.

The hope of salvation: While Jesus speaks often about the reality of hell, He also offered hope and salvation to those who turn to Him. In John 3:16, He says that whoever believes in Him will not perish but have eternal life. In John 11:25–26, He says, "I am the resurrection and the life. Whoever believes in me, though he dies, yet shall he live, and everyone who lives and believes in me shall never die."

In conclusion, Jesus speaks of hell as a place of eternal punishment and separation from God for those who reject Him. He urged His listeners to repent and turn to God in order to avoid the punishment of hell. However, He also offered hope and salvation to all who believe in Him.

CHAPTER 33

Jesus Describes Heaven

JESUS SPEAKS OFTEN about heaven, describing it as a place of eternal life and joy in the presence of God. In the Gospel of John, Jesus tells his disciples, "In my Father's house are many rooms. If it were not so, would I have told you that I go to prepare a place for you?" (John 14:2).

Jesus also speaks of heaven as a place of reward for those who faithfully serve God. In the Sermon on the Mount, he says, "Blessed are you when others revile you and persecute you and utter all kinds of evil against you falsely on my account. Rejoice and be glad, for your reward is great in heaven, for so they persecuted the prophets who were before you" (Matt. 5:11–12).

Jesus also speaks of the importance of seeking heaven above all else. He tells a rich young man, "Sell all that you have and distribute to the poor, and you will have treasure in heaven; and come, follow me" (Luke 18:22). In another passage, he says, "Do not lay up for yourselves treasures on earth, where moth and rust destroy and where thieves break in and steal, but lay up for yourselves treasures in heaven, where neither moth nor rust destroys and where thieves do not break in and steal" (Matt. 6:19–20).

Throughout his teachings, Jesus emphasizes that heaven is not just a future destination, but a present reality for those who follow Him. He tells His disciples, "Truly, truly, I say to you, whoever hears my word and believes him who sent me has eternal life. He does not come into judgment, but has passed from death to life" (John 5:24).

In summary, Jesus speaks of heaven as a place of eternal life and reward for those who serve God faithfully. He also emphasizes the importance of seeking heaven above all else and living in light of its reality in the present.

Will we know each other in heaven? The Bible does not provide a clear answer to the question of whether we will know each other in heaven. However, there are some passages that provide some insight into this topic.

One of the most cited passages is 1 Corinthians 13:12, which says, "For now we see only a reflection as in a mirror; then we shall see face to face. Now I know in part; then I shall know fully, even as I am fully known." This passage suggests that in heaven, we will know each other fully, just as God knows us.

Another passage that provides some insight is Matthew 8:11, which says, "I say to you that many will come from the east and the west, and will take their places at the feast with Abraham, Isaac, and Jacob in the kingdom of heaven." This passage suggests that we will recognize and be with our loved ones in heaven, as Abraham, Isaac, and Jacob are mentioned by name.

Furthermore, Revelation 21:4 says, "He will wipe every tear from their eyes. There will be no more death or mourning or crying or pain, for the old order of things has passed away." This passage suggests that we will have a perfect understanding in heaven and will not experience the pain of separation or loss.

While the Bible does not provide a definitive answer to the question of whether we will know each other in heaven, these passages suggest that we will recognize and be with our loved ones and have a perfect understanding of one another. Ultimately, we can trust in God's plan for our eternal life and rest in the hope of being reunited with our loved ones in His presence.

INDEX

D

E

M

N

O

P

T

U

V

W

A conclusion in a poem about the teachings of Jesus:

In the teachings of Jesus, we find
A path to follow, a way to bind
Our hearts to God, our souls to grace,
And live our lives in love's embrace.

He showed us how to love each other,
To care for one another as a brother,
To serve with joy, to give with grace,
And seek God's wisdom in every place.

He taught us to be humble and kind,
To leave our worries and fears behind,
And trust in God's unfailing love,
As we journey through life above.

He showed us how to find true peace,
In the midst of turmoil and disease,
To rest in Him and His great plan,
And know that all things are in His hand.

And in His life, He gave us hope,
That even in death, we can cope,
For He rose again, triumphant and true,
And opened the way for me and you.

So let us follow His teachings bright,
And walk with Him in love and light,
For in His grace, we find true rest,
And in His love, we know we are blessed.
By Ray Martinez

Other books by Ray Martinez:

A Matter of Survival, Your Fight Against Burglars, about how to protect yourself from burglaries and personal attacks
ISBN 0-9644652-0-5
Saturday's Opinion, a collection of short stories ranging from national, state, and local issues ISBN 0-9644652-2-1
Baby Boy-R, a memoir about Ray Martinez finding his biological mother only to discover she was a victim and thought he had died—yet finding other siblings he never knew
ISBN 978-0-595-44746-6
Growing Daily, a daily guide for daily living and learning what God teaches us each day
ISBN 9781414115436
Just Another Opinion, a collection of short stories on issues ranging from national to local issues and a second sequel to *Saturday's Opinion*
ISBN 978-0-9644652-8-2
From Darkness to Light: The Mai Tran Journey of Passion, a true story of a fifteen-year-old boy's escape from Vietnam as one of the boat people in the seventies
ISBN 978-0-9644652-6-8
The Truth About Marijuana: America's Snake Oil. Today, we are faced with the twenty-first century "snake oil" that proponents want you to believe that marijuana cures everything. Snake oil never lives up to the sellers' hype.
ISBN 978-1-4771-0532-0
Jesus Said, a book that captures some of the key biblical verses and expounds on my personal thoughts and experiences ISBN 978-145357788-2
101 Seeds: Planting and Germinating Greatness. This publication contains heartfelt moments of reflections that inspired me over the years. It is a daily devotion for guidance and peace of mind.
ISBN: 978-1-68314-487-8

Additional books are listed at www.raymartinez.com or https://rayforcouncil.com/consulting/books/

Books that Ray Martinez has been included in

The Death Merchant by Joseph C. Goulden
ISBN 0-671-49341-8
Manhunt, The Incredible Pursuit of CIA Agent Turned Terrorist by Peter Maas
ISBN 0-394-55293-8
101 Memorable Men of Northern Colorado by Arlene Ahlbrandt
ISBN 0-9663932-8-7
Modern visions along the Poudre Valley by Phil Walker
ISBN 1-887982-13-2
Hit From Behind...Out of Perfect Timing Came Perfect Chaos... by Jim Heckel
ISBN 978-1-60791-034-3
50 Interviews—Dream It, Live It, Love It by Don McGrath
ISBN 978-0-98229-071-2
The Blueprint: How the Democrats Won Colorado by Adam Schrager and Rob Witwer
ISBN 978-1-936218-00-4

You can learn more about Ray Martinez at www.raymartinez.com or e-mail raymartinez31@gmail.com, Telephone: 970.690.3686

Ingram Content Group UK Ltd.
Milton Keynes UK
UKHW040958100523
421436UK00028B/375/J

9 781669 874126